BRITAIN IN PICTURES
THE BRITISH PEOPLE IN PICTURES

BOY SCOUTS

GENERAL EDITOR
W. J. TURNER

BOY SCOUTS

E. E. REYNOLDS

WITH
4 PLATES IN COLOUR
4 PLATES IN SEPIA
AND
30 ILLUSTRATIONS IN
BLACK & WHITE

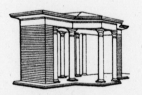

COLLINS · 14 ST. JAMES'S PLACE · LONDON

MCMXLVI

PRODUCED BY
ADPRINT LIMITED LONDON

FIRST PUBLISHED 1944
THIRD IMPRESSION (REVISED) 1946

PRINTED IN GREAT BRITAIN BY
CLARKE & SHERWELL LTD NORTHAMPTON
ON MELLOTEX BOOK PAPER MADE BY
TULLIS RUSSELL & CO LTD MARKINCH SCOTLAND

LIST OF ILLUSTRATIONS

BLACK AND WHITE ILLUSTRATIONS

SHORT BIBLIOGRAPHY

Lord Baden-Powell : *Scouting for Boys*, Pearsons.   *The Wolf Cub's Handbook*, Pearsons
and *Rovering to Success*, Jenkins
E. E. Reynolds : *Baden-Powell*, Oxford University Press

A SCOUT
Pencil drawing by J. H. Dowd

THE COMING OF THE BOY SCOUTS

For most people the words "Boy Scout" call up a picture of a bare-kneed boy wearing a cowboy hat and carrying a pole, or they recall the idea of the daily Good Deed—a theme of good-natured jokes by Ministers of the Crown and Variety Stars. Most would say that Scouting is a "Good Thing," though few of the many well-wishers could give a clear account of the principles and methods of the Boy Scout Movement, or of how it has developed. The story can be given here in bare outline only, but it is one which should be widely known, for the Boy Scout Movement is one of Britain's most characteristic contributions to the world of the Twentieth Century.

Consider the following facts—In 1939 there were, in round figures, 400,000 boys and young men in the Boy Scouts in Great Britain with 40,000 adults concerned with their training ; there were 600,000 members of the Movement in other parts of the British Empire ; to this must be added another two and a half million in forty-nine foreign countries. It is impossible to calculate how many present day adults have had some Scout training, but as the Movement has now been active for more than a generation, there must be many millions of men throughout the world who owe something to the Boy Scouts; so too there must be a vast number of women who have passed through the Girl Guides, a movement whose principles and methods are, *mutatis mutandis*, the same as those of the Boy Scouts.

All this began in an experimental way with a man camping on an island with twenty boys in 1907. For as with most social movements, Scouting was not born out of a Blue Book or Survey ; nor was any Committee bidden to find a Leader, still less to train one. Scouting began with a man. Like Lord Shaftesbury, or Dr. Barnardo, Robert Baden-Powell (1857-1941) was simply tackling a problem which came his way without any idea of beginning anything on a large scale.

The camp on Brownsea Island was not the beginning of the ideas behind the Boy Scout Movement. We can trace their origin right back to B.-P.'s own boyhood experiences. He was the fifth of six brothers who were encouraged to spend their leisure out of doors camping and boating. Soon after he went to Charterhouse, the school moved to the country, and the woods (placed out of bounds) became a happy hunting-ground for the boy who was already developing three characteristics which the years strengthened : an independence of spirit, a love of watching animals and of all woodcraft, and a longing for intervals of solitude in the midst of a very active life.

As a subaltern in India, he quickly discovered that his abilities lay in the field of scouting, surveying and reconnaissance. Soon his genius as an instructor found play in teaching the elements of these subjects to young soldiers many of whom could not read or write. It was then that he experimented with the methods later to be the framework of Boy Scout training—the use of the small groups of half-a-dozen men under their own leader as the unit for instruction, for competitions and for games. Here he broke away from more orthodox army methods.

India was followed by varied experience of secret service work in the Mediterranean, fighting Zulus in S. Africa, pioneering and scouting in Ashanti, and then by his memorable scouting achievements in Matabeleland. It was in this last experience that he made his name as the greatest of all army scouts, and in after years he was able to base many a talk to boys on incidents drawn from his nights in the Matopo Hills of what is now Southern Rhodesia.

At the age of forty he again went out to India, this time as Colonel of the 5th Dragoon Guards. He formed and trained a body of regimental Scouts and in so doing developed still further the methods he had used

PORTRAIT OF LORD BADEN-POWELL 1857-1941
Water colour by Ape Junior from *Vanity Fair*
By courtesy of the Boy Scouts Imperial Headquarters

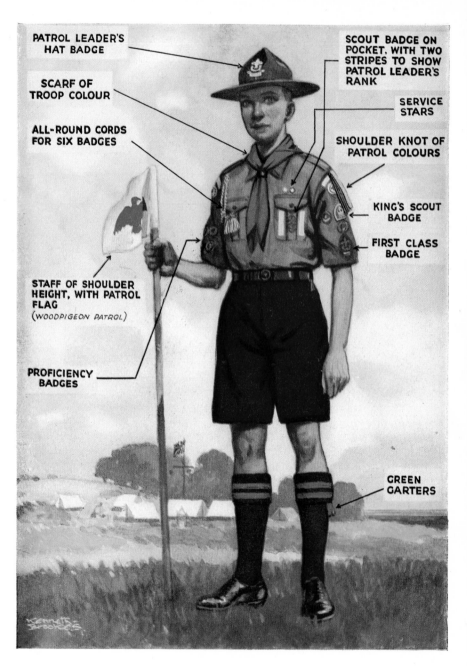

PATROL LEADER'S
HAT BADGE

SCARF OF
TROOP COLOUR

ALL-ROUND CORDS
FOR SIX BADGES

STAFF OF SHOULDER
HEIGHT, WITH PATROL
FLAG
(WOODPIGEON PATROL)

PROFICIENCY
BADGES

SCOUT BADGE ON
POCKET, WITH TWO
STRIPES TO SHOW
PATROL LEADER'S
RANK

SERVICE
STARS

SHOULDER KNOT OF
PATROL COLOURS

KING'S SCOUT
BADGE

FIRST CLASS
BADGE

GREEN
GARTERS

BOY SCOUT UNIFORM AND BADGES
Water Colour by Kenneth Brookes, 1943
By courtesy of the Boy Scouts Imperial Headquarters

in earlier years, for he now had his own practical experience to draw upon. The instruction was summed up in a small handbook, *Aids to Scouting*, which was published at a time when the name of Baden-Powell had become that of a national hero.

Just before war began in South Africa in 1899, B.-P. was sent out to organise an irregular frontier force, and it was with part of this company that he was besieged in Mafeking. All his special abilities now had full scope ; his resourcefulness was constantly needed to improvise new ways of deceiving a clever enemy ; his night scouting kept him informed of movements of men and guns, and that quick good humour of his prevented the besieged from getting depressed for he could both be the man in command and also unbend to play the fool in a mock circus or at a concert. Mafeking was important for the future Boy Scout Movement since it was then that B.-P. realised how boys will rise to responsibility when it is put upon them. A corps of boys was organised in the town as messengers and they rendered valuable service.

B.-P. became the hero of boys everywhere, and he was soon over-whelmed with letters asking for advice from his young admirers. When he returned to England, this hero-worship was intensified. He also discovered to his amazement that his military manual, *Aids to Scouting*, was being used as a source of ideas by some teachers. Then he was invited to review a rally of the Boys' Brigade and he met its founder, Sir William Smith. B.-P. was tremendously impressed and he was anxious to help. He felt that possibly scouting and other outdoor activities might attract more boys to the Brigade. Sir William encouraged him to work out a scheme, and for a time this was used by those Brigade officers who were attracted by the method. The camp on Brownsea Island in 1907 was an experiment to see how boys liked the ideas, and out of this came *Scouting for Boys* which was written with Sir William Smith's encourage-ment. Then the storm broke ! Although the scheme was intended as an auxiliary method of training for the Boys' Brigade or for any organisations who cared to use it, boys outside these bought the fortnightly parts of the book and began "Scouting" on their own. They found Scoutmasters, and men who were captured by the book collected boys together to form Troops.

So a separate movement was created in spite of B.-P.'s original in-tentions, and its progress has been continuous. The relations with the Boys' Brigade have remained most friendly and the two have developed side by side with the greatest good will.

BADEN-POWELL WITH SOME RHODESIAN SCOUTS

PRINCIPLES AND METHODS

The aim of the Movement is to provide opportunities for developing those qualities of character which make the good citizen—a man of honour, self-disciplined and self-reliant, willing and able to serve the community.

There is nothing new in the aim ; long ago it was stated by Plato as "education in virtue from youth upwards, which makes a man passionately desire to be the perfect citizen, and teaches him how rightly to rule and how to obey."

Scouting is distinguished by its methods. These are based on the normal desires of the boy. By giving practical and attractive outlets for them, Scouting turns them to socially valuable purposes. The boy is unaware of much that lies behind his training ; to him it is a great game played with his comrades as campers, pioneers and frontiersmen.

The boy is set a standard of conduct for his guidance. This is stated in the Scout Law :

(1) A Scout's honour is to be trusted.

(2) A Scout is loyal to the King, his Country, his Scouters, his Parents, his Employers, and to those under him.

(3) A Scout's duty is to be useful, and to help others.

KING GEORGE V WITH LORD BADEN-POWELL INSPECTING BOY SCOUTS, 1920

(4) A Scout is a friend to all, and a brother to every other Scout, no matter to what country, class or creed the other may belong.

(5) A Scout is courteous.

(6) A Scout is a friend to animals.

(7) A Scout obeys orders of his Parents, Patrol Leader, or Scoutmaster, without question.

(8) A Scout smiles and whistles under all difficulties.

(9) A Scout is thrifty.

(10) A Scout is clean in thought, word and deed.

This Law is not a series of "DONT'S," but a positive statement of decent behaviour. When a boy becomes a Scout he promises to do his best to live up to this standard. The full Promise is as follows :

"On my honour I promise that I will do my best :

(1) To do my duty to God, and the King.

(2) To help other people at all times.

(3) To obey the Scout Law."

The order of these is important. "Duty to God" is the basis of religion, and while the Scout Movement itself is not committed to any one creed, the boys are encouraged to fulfil their obligations if they are already Church members, or to accept such obligations by becoming members. In camp, arrangements are made, where possible, for attendance at Church or Chapel, and where this is not practicable, a Scouts' Own is held in camp. This policy has been approved by the leaders of the Churches who have welcomed the co-operation of the Boy Scouts Association.

"Duty to the King" sums up in a phrase that sense of responsibility to the community which it is the aim of Scouting to develop.

The "Daily Good Turn" is the first step towards learning how "to help other people at all times." By this simple means it is hoped that a *habit* of thinking unselfishly may be formed, and the fact that this is perhaps the best known feature of Scouting proves its effectiveness. How successful this has been is fully shown by the long list of varied kinds of National Service undertaken by many thousands of Scouts. The Law and Promise are not taught so much by word of mouth as by the whole scheme of practical training. Boys learn by doing more than by listening, but all the activities of Scouting are directed by the spirit of the Law and Promise. The boy disciplines himself in striving to attain the ideal set before him.

Scouting in practice assumes that the boy can, and should, be trusted. Once he has taken his Promise, he is trusted to carry it out to the best of his ability. The distinctive method of Scouting is known as the Patrol System. The boys of a Troop are divided into small units or Patrols of six to eight boys each under a Patrol Leader who is given considerable responsibility in the training of the members of his Patrol, and with the other Patrol Leaders, in the general organisation of the Troop. All the Patrol Leaders form a Court of Honour which meets regularly to plan the Troop's activities, to discuss finance, and to watch over the general progress made by the Scouts.

OUR YOUNGEST LINE OF DEFENCE
Boy Scout to Mrs. Britannia : *Fear not, Gran'ma,*
no danger can befall you now, remember I am with you
Pen drawing by Sir Bernard Partridge, from *Punch*, 1909

It should also be noted that the Patrol System satisfies that gang instinct which leads boys to combine together in "secret societies" sometimes harmlessly but sometimes with bad results. Scouting canalises this instinct and turns it to socially useful purposes.

"The gang" is not looking for mischief, but for romance and adventure, and Scouting offers these with its uniform and its outdoor activities. The uniform is well known but the accompanying explanatory picture may be useful ; it was designed for outdoor life to give the maximum of freedom with that smartness of appearance and touch of colour which appeals to the growing boy. It was, in 1908, a daring, and even revolutionary, kind of dress.

A scheme of badges lures the Scout on from one practical achievement to another. As a result of following this trail, he should develop into a

SCOUTS MAKING A SHELTER

fellow on whose word others can rely, one able to look after himself, resourceful in any emergency and able (not merely willing) to help others. There are two groups of badges—those for efficiency and those for proficiency. All Scouts have to undergo the tests for efficiency, but each may make his own choice of the proficiency badges.

There are three efficiency badges—Tenderfoot, Second Class, and First Class. Some idea of the scope may be gathered from an outline of the tests for First Class. The Scout must have had good experience of camping, and must be able to swim, to deal with common emergencies and accidents, and send messages by Morse or Semaphore. He must show his powers of observation and deduction by a tracking test, and he must have some knowledge of trees and birds. His pioneering knowledge includes knotting, lashing and splicing, tree felling and trimming. His final test is a 24-hour journey of at least fourteen miles during which he must find his way by map, pitch his tent, cook his meals, and all the time keep a log of his journey which must include a sketch-map of his route.

In addition to taking these tests of efficiency there are a number of Proficiency Badges. Certain of these are known as King's Scout Badges as they are particularly intended as Public Service training: the most important of these are Ambulance Man, Handyman, Pathfinder, Public

14

SEA SCOUTS PRACTISING LASHING

Health Man, and Rescuer. Another group of badges encourages the Scout to specialise in those outdoor activities which are particularly distinctive of Scouting ; such badges are the Explorer, Stalker, Tracker, Forester, Naturalist, Pioneer, and Weatherman.

The rest of the Proficiency Badges are intended to encourage each boy to develop a skill or hobby which may or may not help him to choose a livelihood, but which will certainly provide him with pleasant leisure-time pursuits ; only a few can be given here as examples : Artist, Book-binder, Camper, Carpenter, Cook, Electrician, Engineer, Gardener, Musician, Photographer, Prospector, Starman and Wireless-man.

Throughout the training great attention is given to health, and each Scout is made personally responsible for his own health and physical development. This is not done so much through formal P.T. as through the training in healthy habits, camp life, Scouting games and other out-door activities. A simple system of six exercises is taught, and these the boy is encouraged to practise each morning on getting out of bed. He is not expected to develop big muscles or to perform complicated exercises, but is shown that health is a matter of good bodily habits, natural exercise, with simple food and sound sleep. Camp life underlines the value of these things.

EXPANSION

It has already been explained that B.-P.'s original idea was to provide a system of attractive activities which could be used in any Boys' Brigade, Club, or other boys' organisation. This modest intention was quickly shattered by facts. The number of boys doing Boy Scouting on their own grew so rapidly that some kind of organisation was obviously necessary. So with great daring, a small office was opened and a stock of twelve Scout hats was laid in, with a similarly cautious amount of other equipment. (In 1938, some 30,000 hats were sold in the Scout Shop.)

Numbers, however, soon overwhelmed all such timid arrangements. By 1910 there were over 100,000 Boy Scouts in the United Kingdom alone. B.-P. found it necessary to give up all idea of a further army career in order to take in hand the organisation and development of this rapidly growing Movement.

There were extensions in several directions. At the first big rally in 1909 at the Crystal Palace, B.-P. (who paraded in General's full uniform) was startled to see some girls present who insisted that they were Girl Scouts. Something clearly had to be done about them, and so the Girl Guides came into existence.

Other arrivals were small brothers and their friends who wanted to be Scouts, but their diminutive size brought ridicule on the bigger boys as well as restricting their activities. Out of this difficulty arose the Wolf Cub section. Here B.-P. made ingenious use of Kipling's *Jungle Books* as an imaginative framework.

The importance of this youngest section is considerable ; during the war years attention was largely concentrated on the 14-18 year-olds, and there was a tendency to overlook the fact that successful later training must be based on successful early training.

After some years the original Boy Scouts grew older and wanted to retain their connexion with the Movement, so a new section—the Rover Scouts —was formed. Some of them have become Scouters (a general name for officers), others have acted as Instructors or have helped to run Scout Camping Grounds. At special times they have proved of great service to the Movement while at the same time continuing their training as citizens.

B.-P.'s eldest brother, Warington, was a keen yachtsman, and he had taken his younger brothers on many a boating expedition. It was therefore natural that B.-P. should want to form a Sea Scout branch for boys who felt the call of the sea. Warington B.-P. wrote the official handbook. The Boy Scouts are the proud owners of Captain Scott's ship *Discovery*. It is now moored in the Thames off Temple Pier and serves as a training centre for Sea Scouts.

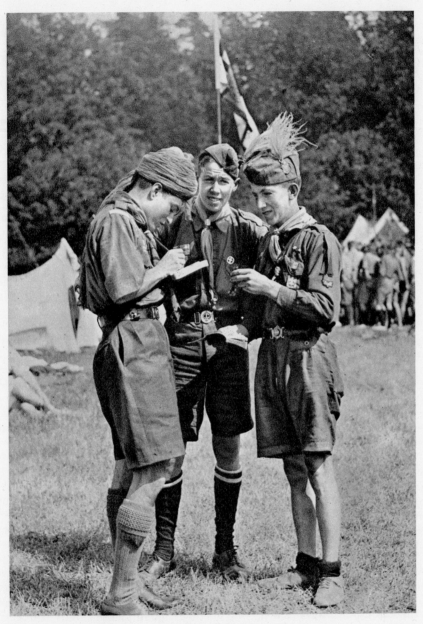

An International Rover Camp in Sweden, 1935
Rover Scouts of India and Norway

WOLF CUBS
At the Jamboree held in Holland in 1937

Other special needs have been met as they arose ; two may here be mentioned as examples. The Deep-Sea Scouts is a scheme by which a former Scout who goes to sea can get into touch with the Scout representatives at ports all over the world ; it is hardly necessary to point out how valuable such a linking-up can be to a lad who has just left home and is plunged into a strange life. The second need is that of the boy who is physically handicapped and may have to spend much time in hospital. Scouting comes to him in a form adapted to suit his limitations and he learns to feel that he can, after all, share some of the activities of those who are fully fit. Doctors have testified to the psychological value of this kind of Good Deed.

Such have been the expansions of the original scheme to satisfy growing demands. A note has already been made of the expansion beyond Great Britain. There is nothing very surprising in the spread of Scouting to the Dominions, but it has proved of equal—possibly of greater—value in colonies and protectorates and even in such a remote island as Tristan da Cunha.

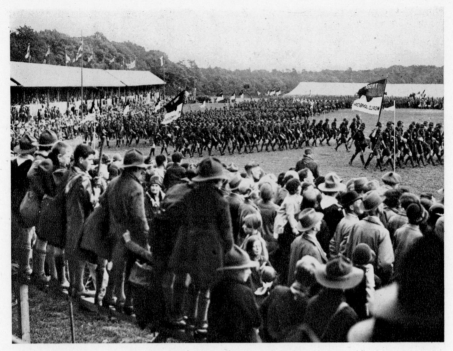

MARCH PAST OF THE NATIONS
At the Jamboree held at Arrowe Park in 1929

The methods of Scouting have proved adaptable to the varied needs of boys of many races, for neither colour nor creed is a bar. Probably the Movement has gone as far as is practicable at present in bringing together boys of different colours. Scouting, generally speaking, keeps them in separate Troops for their training and brings them together on certain occasions when they can all feel that they are members of one Movement.

In the matter of creed, Scouting has again adopted a practical policy which has made it possible for all sections of the Christian community as well as of other religious communities to work happily side by side without conflict. This has been achieved by insisting that each member has a duty to God to perform which he is expected to carry out according to the instructions of his spiritual teachers and guides. Where this policy is loyally carried out, there has rarely been any difficulty. For boys who do not belong to any religious body—an increasing number—there is still the guidance of the Scout Law, and for them there is a simple service called a Scouts' Own. Few experiences are more memorable than a

Scouts' Own held out of doors in camp ; the joining together in plainly expressed prayers, the singing of the hymns and the short talk on some aspect of the Scout Law help to produce the atmosphere in which religious faith can grow.

No attempt was made to urge foreign countries to accept the method ; when the Nazis suppressed the Movement in the Netherlands—as they did also in other occupied countries—they gave as one reason that the Boy Scouts were "an instrument of English influence." The truth is that foreign countries began Boy Scouts without any urging. Naturally visitors interested in the training of boys studied the working of the Movement here, just as foreigners studied the Hitler Youth before 1939. Sometimes a private citizen of another country read *Scouting for Boys* by chance, and this persuaded him to try the method at home—with the astonishing result that in a year or two he found himself head of a large organisation !

The explanation is that B.-P. had discovered certain principles and methods of universal application in the training of boys ; these could be easily adjusted to meet the particular circumstances of any country from Iceland to New Zealand, and round the world from China to Peru.

The Movement expanded in another direction. In 1919 Gilwell Park, a beautiful estate on the edge of Epping Forest near Chingford, was presented to the Association as a camping ground. It was found to be particularly suitable also as a training centre for Scoutmasters. B.-P. at once saw the possibilities and since that day a system of training has grown up which has spread all over the world. It had the marks of individuality that one always expected with B.-P.'s work. The obvious way to run a Training Course is to give lectures, but B.-P. wanted to achieve something more than just giving information. He, therefore, laid it down that the Training Course would be run in camp with the Scoutmasters forming a Scout Troop, or in the case of Cubmasters, a Cub Pack.

The Scoutmasters are divided into Patrols, each Patrol having its own tent and cooking place. The members of the Patrol take it in turn to carry out the different jobs which are normally done by the boys : thus each Scoutmaster is for one day the Patrol Leader, on another day the cook, and on another day he may be the general errand boy of the Patrol.

As far as possible instruction is put into practice to make quite sure that the training of the boy is also kept very practical and very active. Thus the Scoutmasters not only play various games, practice tracking, and learn the use of the axe, but they finish up their Course with a 24-hour hike in Epping Forest when they take with them all the necessary gear for the night. On their return they hand in reports of the journey with sketch maps and so on. For successful Scoutmasters, B.-P. decided that there should be a special award of what he named the Wood Badge. This consisted of a couple of beads from a necklace which he captured in one of the minor Zulu wars. Now, of course, that more than 15,000

CAMP FIRE CIRCLE AND TRAINING GROUND AT GILWELL PARK
Water colour by Kenneth Brookes, 1943

men and women have earned the Badge, replicas of the originals are used. But before gaining the badge, the Scoutmaster must also pass a Theoretical Course done by correspondence to ensure that he knows the chief principles and methods of the Movement thoroughly. There is also a third and final part which is the practical application of his training to the work of the Troop, and here his District Commissioner has to certify that he has proved that his training has been of value and that he can apply it sensibly.

It was not long before Scoutmasters from other parts of the British Empire and also from foreign countries began to come to Gilwell to go through this training. These men then returned to their own countries and started similar systems worked on the same principles as at Gilwell. They have started training centres, sometimes naming them Gilwell, modelled on the parent Training Camp. In this country it has been possible to acquire other camping and training centres. An interesting example of this is the Youlbury Training Camp, which was given to the Movement by Sir Arthur Evans, himself a very enthusiastic supporter of the Boy Scouts.

ORGANISATION

B.-P. often said, "We are a Movement, not an Organisation." By it he meant two things; that there is plenty of latitude in Scouting for meeting local conditions and personal aptitude, and secondly that organisation is a means to an end, and not an end in itself.

Obviously some kind of organisation must exist to prevent chaos, but the Boy Scouts have, on the whole, avoided becoming entangled in too much red tape. In fact it is true to say that the Scoutmaster has a wide field for exercising his own likes and dislikes and for developing his ideas and for experimenting. There is no doubt that this freedom of action has been a source of strength as it has prevented any stereotyped form of Scouting from being formed. It has, of course, its weaknesses since there is a wide variety in the quality of Scout work. The gains do, however, far outweigh the losses.

The organisation is based on the principle of decentralisation. The Headquarters works through the Counties, and they work through the Districts who in turn work through the Local Associations composed of a number of Groups.

The most important adult is the Scoutmaster ; historically he came before the Commissioner whose job is not similar to that of an Inspecting Officer, but is more that of an adviser.

The Group, when complete, consists of a Wolf Cub Pack (ages 8-11), a Scout Troop (11-18), and a Rover Crew (over 18). Some Groups are attached to Churches, Schools, and other Institutions. These are known as Sponsored Groups and the authority concerned has the right to nominate the Scouters. A Group attached to a Church is therefore assured of a definite religious association, and the boys are encouraged to become active members of the Church. At first sight it would seem that there would be no place for a Scout Troop in a School, but experience shows that it can supply a kind of training in outdoor living and in resourcefulness which is beyond the scope of most schools.

A Group Committee is a valuable aid to the life of the Group ; on this are representatives of the parents, and this safeguards Group property and finance as well as supplying continuity if a Scouter has to give up through moving from the District, or for some other good reason.

Finance is always a problem in voluntary organisations. The principle in Scouting is that each unit looks after itself from Headquarters down to the Group. Lavish gifts have often proved dangerous, and the general rule of the Group earning its funds is sound. Various methods are adopted —such as concerts or dramatic entertainments, or work days when each Scout gets a job of work such as clipping a hedge, or weeding the garden, and hands over the proceeds to the Group. Sometimes it is difficult to

THEIR MAJESTIES, THE KING AND QUEEN, WITH THE PRINCESSES, INSPECTING BOYS WHO
HAVE BECOME SCOUTS DESPITE PHYSICAL HANDICAPS

find the money for uniforms, so these may be provided by the Group and then paid for by weekly subscriptions. Begging for funds is forbidden though most Groups have a few annual subscribers who are supporters without being active members.

There is indeed a big field in Scouting for the layman. The Local Association needs support not only by funds, but by the voluntary help of a chairman, treasurer and secretary. Then anyone who has some special skill can be used as an instructor for a hobby, or as an examiner for the appropriate badge. The more laymen who can be roped in for these jobs, the more can the Scouters devote themselves to their main business —the training of the boy.

23

ZEBRA AND LION
Pen drawing by Lord Baden-Powell

ACTIVITIES

The earlier reference to the badges will have given some idea as to what Boy Scouts do, but the general reader must be sometimes puzzled to know exactly what are the activities of the Boy Scouts and what they do in their mysterious meetings. So it will perhaps not be amiss to describe a typical Troop Meeting. Space will not allow similar descriptions for meetings of Wolf Cubs and of Rover Scouts, but apart from their special purpose it will be true to say that the general idea is the same.

First for the Troop Meeting indoors. This sounds paradoxical since Scouting is primarily an outdoor Movement, but unfortunately in this country we have to meet on dark evenings during the winter and under weather conditions which are not always favourable to outdoor activities. There is, of course, always the danger that a Scout Troop may become too much of an indoor club and this calls for constant vigilance.

Every Group aims at having its own Headquarters. This may be something quite unpretentious like an old garage or stables, or indeed anywhere where there are four walls and a reasonably weather-proof roof. The important point is that the boys should feel that it is a place that belongs to themselves where they can do what they like, which they can decorate in their own way to suit their fancy, and where they can store their gear. Unfortunately, many Groups have to be content with the use of a Village Hall or schoolroom and this very much limits the activities. The present move to put up Youth Centres all over the country which can be shared by the various Youth Movements is of doubtful wisdom if by that is meant that the individual organisations will not also have their own separate places. A central place which may provide such amenities as a swimming bath, gymnasium, a hall for dramatic performances, etc., may well be desirable but it is also very important that for Scouting at any rate each Group should have a place that it can call its very own.

When the Troop assembles the visitor will notice that the boys have collected in four or five small groups, each containing six or seven boys. These are the Patrols and it will be noticed throughout that the activities are worked on a Patrol basis and that the Patrol

ANIMALS OF THE AFRICAN VELDT
Water colour by Lord Baden-Powell

DESIGN FOR SCOUTS ENROLMENT CARD
Water colour by Lord Baden-Powell
By courtesy of the Boy Scouts Imperial Headquarters

Leader plays a very important part in everything which is done. The first item of the meeting will be the breaking of the Union Flag, followed by an inspection. This is not allowed to take up much time but does just ensure that degree of smartness and correctness of uniform, personal cleanliness, etc., which is important in the training of the boy. This inspection will probably be followed by some very active games. The boys have either been shut up in school all day or at work in a factory or elsewhere, and they need an opportunity for letting off steam, and so they will be given a full chance of doing this with as much noise as they like for ten minutes before they settle down to more serious work. The range of games that can be played is very considerable so that there is no need for constant repetition of the same game. Most Troops, however, seem to have certain games which become their own special favourites.

The next item will probably be some practice in one of the activities included in the Scout Tests. For instance, it may include signalling or knotting, or there may be a period for the Patrols to get together to have instruction from their own Patrol Leaders in preparation for a competition or just to get them further along in their Scout Tests.

The next important item will probably be an Inter-Patrol competition. For instance, arrangements may be made beforehand for a friend of the Scoutmaster's to burst into the hall and pretend to throw a fit in the middle of it. The way in which the boys deal with such a sudden emergency will be watched very carefully by the Scoutmaster and later on he will point out mistakes which were made and praise any particularly good effort of one of the Patrols. The competition, however, may be something much more straightforward, such as splicing a rope, or a set test in First Aid, or possibly a test in observation. A great deal of emphasis is put on developing the powers of observation and one of the commonest forms is known as Kim's Game as it was derived from the book of that title by Kipling. (The curious reader should see Chapter IX.) The boy is shown a collection of a dozen or so small articles and after a minute's observation, he has to make a list of the objects. At a later stage, he has to describe them as well. The competition may be followed by an instructional talk from one of the Scoutmasters on pioneering or some such subject. Here he will be following B.-P.'s own method which he used at Brownsea Island when he would give a talk round the camp fire at night in preparation for the next day's activities. This yarn will not take long and will be usually followed by another game, after which the meeting will conclude with prayers and the lowering of the Flag.

It must not be thought that this is a fixed routine for all Troops. They are encouraged to vary their programmes very considerably and to plan them carefully so that in the course of a period of months they do make very definite progress. This planning of the work should be done by the

KIM'S GAME

Patrol Leaders together with the Scouters in a meeting which is known as a Court of Honour. This is a very important part of the training of a Scout because he learns quite early to meet together with his fellows and to work out plans for the future. In this way he learns that he cannot always have his own way and that there is a good deal of give and take in life.

There may be other evening meetings in the week, for instance, an evening for badge work. Here the visitor if he came into the Troop Room, or, if the Troop is lucky, into the special workshop, would see some Scouts busy making toys, others doing leather work which may either take the form of making things like belts or knife sheaths or doing something purely utilitarian like mending a pair of boots, other Scouts may be learning how to bind books and applying this to the books in their own Troop Library, yet another group may be having instruction in carpentry or in simple electrical work, and so on. This reference to hobbies and activities emphasises how important it is for the Troop to have its own place where it can do these things.

PRACTICE IN MORSE SIGNALLING

In the winter months the Troop may be busy preparing for a concert or for the performance of a play. This will call for all kinds of practical ability and those Scouts who are perhaps not suited for taking part in the performance as actors or singers will be equally busy and equally enthusiastic in making the properties, or rigging up the stage, or making and painting the scenery. Most Troops do have some kind of annual show which is as far as possible made a useful part of their training.

In addition to the evening meetings, Troops try to arrange for Saturday afternoons out of doors, even during the winter. This will give opportunities for applying things learned indoors, perhaps only in theory, such as fire lighting, cooking, tracking, learning to recognise trees, and so on. Or the afternoon may take the form of what is known in the Movement as a wide game. This is really a development of the better-known field day of such organisations as Cadets. The wide game is carried out over as big a stretch of country as possible, though for the town Troops it may have to be adapted to the streets and a park. The framework of the game may be quite simple such as, for instance, capturing flags from

REFUGEE FRENCH SCOUTS IN CAMP IN ENGLAND, 1941
Preparing a meal

an opponent's camp, or it may be worked out in a more elaborate form as a story of Red Indians, or a tale such as John Buchan's *John Macnab* may be used as a kind of theme. These games are, of course, so arranged that they bring in a number of practical activities such as Ambulance work and Signalling, as well as the more obvious skills in stalking and tracking.

But above all, *the* Scouting activity is camping. Some hardened Scouts will camp practically all the year round and they are encouraged to do so once they have gained the necessary skill and knowledge, but for the younger Scouts, especially, camping will begin about Easter time and will last through the summer months. There will be week-end camps, possibly at one of the Scout Headquarters camp sites like Gilwell Park, lasting from Saturday afternoon to Sunday evening. Every Troop aims at having ten days or a fortnight in camp in the summer, usually in August. Here again Scouting has its own methods ; each Patrol works as a unit and does its own cooking and looks after itself as much as possible. This

THE JAMBOREE CAMP IN HOLLAND, 1937
At this camp 28,000 Scouts of 31 nations camped together

is deliberately intended as a training in self-reliance so that the boys do not get into the habit of expecting other people to do things for them.

The older Scouts may manage to get a camp or hike abroad in the good days of peace. This practice had developed to a very great extent before 1939 and thousands of Scouts left this country every year to camp or hike on the Continent. A few were lucky enough to get further afield, for instance to Canada, but the expense of such a far-afield expedition was too great for most Troops to face. It is certainly very much to be hoped that now it may be possible again for Scouts to get to more distant places and particularly to America and to parts of the British Empire.

The greatest camps of all have been the Jamborees held every four years in different countries. Here were gathered together Scouts from many nations for a fortnight under canvas. They would get to know each other under conditions which very quickly broke down any reserves that there might be between boys of one nation and another. This, too, is a practice which everyone hopes will be greatly developed in the future.

SCOUTS SCALING A WALL

CITIZENSHIP

It has already been noted that one of the chief purposes of the Scout Movement is the training of boys to be good citizens. B.-P.'s own definition was, "A school of citizenship through woodcraft." When he wrote that in 1908 he was talking a language which few people understood. Since then—and in some degree through his teaching—the notion of training for citizenship has become almost a commonplace. Unfortunately, the idea is often so limited as to mean chiefly having a knowledge of the machinery of local and central government. B.-P.'s notion was something

BUILDING THE LOG CABIN AT GILWELL PARK

much wider and more human—he thought of a citizen as one who is able to look after himself and to live happily with others, and, at the same time, able, as well as willing, to help where help is needed for the good of the community ; and, finally, if called upon, willing to sacrifice much, indeed life itself, for the common good.

This view finds support in Sir Richard Livingstone's *Education for a World Adrift* (1943) where he points out that "Citizenship is not information or intellectual interest, though these are part of it ; it is conduct not theory, action not knowledge, and a man may be familiar with the contents of every book on the social sciences without being a good citizen."

31

ENGLISH SCOUTS IN SWITZERLAND

Later he mentions the "Scout and Guide Movement" (rightly thinking of them as one in aim and method) as "one of the institutions whose members learn the habit of citizenship by being citizens." One or two indications have already been given of how this is done in Scouting, but the subject is so important that more needs to be said.

The code of behaviour set out in the Scout Law is a social code; reference to it will show how the central idea is applied to the benefit of others ; although we are told "a Scout is so-and-so" this positive statement is by no means self-centred. Thus throughout there runs the general theme of making oneself a better individual in order to be a better neighbour.

Such a series of precepts is far from original; where B.-P. broke new ground was in giving a more direct practical, everyday, application. Thus—if "A Scout's duty is to be useful, and help others"—then he will begin straight away with a daily Good Deed ; nothing spectacular, but just something which otherwise he would probably not do. Also he will learn how to give First Aid to the injured, and he will learn to swim and to do rescue work in the water. So one could go on illustrating how B.-P. in his scheme of training skilfully linked up ideals with actions, and over all threw the cloak of romance.

SCOUTS PRACTISING PIONEERING

A SEA SCOUT

A Patrol in Camp

Another aspect of citizenship training is the development of right qualities of character, for the good citizen is first and foremost a man of sound character. The quality above all others developed in Scouting as proved time and time again in war, is self-reliance. This is of growing importance when more and more is being done *for* the boy and less and less *by* him. So in camp he learns to make his own bed (and lie on it), to cook his food (and eat it), and to take his share in the community chores (and put up with it). He learns further to make a little go a long way and to improvise. This is one of the benefits of Scouting which is in constant danger of being smothered by the production by enterprising manufacturers of all kinds of gadgets for camp. But that patent cooker is a danger ; far better for the boy to turn a cocoa tin into a billy and the lid of a biscuit box into a frying pan, as indeed the early Scouts had to do. So Scouting too has its little war against the encroaching "amenities" of "civilisation."

B.-P. was also keen on developing the boy's powers of observation and deduction ; his own experience as a practical Scout gave him a great store of examples from which to draw. Here for instance is the kind of incident he used to quicken the boy's interest :

"I was one day, during the Matabele War, with a native out scouting near to the Matopo Hills over a wide grassy plain. Suddenly we crossed a track freshly made in grass, where the blades of grass were still green and damp, though pressed down ; all were bending one way, which showed the direction in which the people had been travelling ; following up the track for a bit it got on to a patch of sand, and we then saw that it was the spoor of several women (small feet with straight edge, and short steps) and boys (small feet, curved edge, and longer strides), walking, not running, towards the hills, about five miles away ; where we believed the enemy to be hiding.

"Then we saw a leaf lying about ten yards off the track. There were no trees for miles, but we knew that trees having this kind of leaf grew at a village fifteen miles away, in the direction from which the footmarks were coming. It seemed likely therefore that the women had come from that village, bringing the leaf with them, and had gone to the hills.

"On picking up the leaf we found it was damp, and smelled of native beer. The short steps showed that the women were carrying loads. So we guessed that according to the custom they had been carrying pots of native beer on their heads, the mouths of the pots being stopped up with bunches of leaves. One of these leaves had fallen out ; but we found it ten yards off the track, which showed that at the time it fell a wind was blowing. There was no wind now, *i.e.*, seven o'clock, but there had been some about five o'clock.

"So we guessed from all these little signs that a party of women and boys had brought beer during the night from the village fifteen miles away, and had taken it to the enemy on the hills, arriving there soon after six o'clock.

"The men would probably start to drink the beer at once (as it goes sour in a few hours), and would, by the time we could get there, be getting sleepy and keeping a bad look-out, so we should have a favourable chance of looking at their position.

"We accordingly followed the women's track, found the enemy, made our observations, and got away with our information without any difficulty."

That example has been given at length to serve the double purpose of showing what B.-P. meant by observation and deduction and how he taught by using yarns from real life to capture the boys' attention. Most people would think it hopeless to apply such an adventure to the mean streets of an industrial town. But not B.-P. He knew how a boy's

SEA SCOUTS LEARNING TO READ THE COMPASS

vivid imagination can turn an asphalt playground into the African Veldt and a narrow street into Deadman's Gulch.

Then he devised games for the boys to develop their powers of observation. As for example, the game called "Spotting the Spot" in which a series of photos or sketches of objects in the neighbourhood, such as would be known to all the Scouts if they kept their eyes open, have to be identified—such, for instance, as a cross-roads, a curious window, gargoyles or a weathercock, a tree, a reflection in some water caused by a particular building, and so on. A pair of Scouts can play most of the competitions between themselves, if they like; a Patrol Leader can match one pair of his Scouts against another pair in the game, and thus get them practised at it, and when they become really good he can challenge other Patrols to compete against his.

In this as in other games the Patrol method is used—that is the Scouts training each other rather than being trained by an adult instructor. This kind of practice finds its culmination in outdoor afternoons and in camp. Once more the game with its romantic possibilities is the medium used : the example here is called "Smugglers Over the Border."

"The 'Border' is a certain line of country about four hundred yards long, preferably a road or wide path or bit of sand, on which foot-tracks can easily be seen. One Patrol watches the border with sentries posted along this road, with a reserve posted farther inland. This latter about half-way between the 'border' and the 'town' ; the 'town' would be a base marked by a tree, building, or flags, etc., about half a mile distant from the border. A hostile Patrol of smugglers assembles about half a mile on the other side of the border. They will all cross the border, in any formation they please, either singly or together or scattered, and make for the town, either walking or running, or at scout pace. Only one among them is supposed to be smuggling, and he wears tracking irons, so that the sentries walk up and down their beat (they may not run till after the 'alarm'), waiting for the tracks of the smuggler. Directly a sentry sees the track, he gives the alarm signal to the reserve and starts himself to follow up the track as fast as he can. The reserve thereupon co-operate with them and try to catch the smuggler before he can reach the town. Once within the boundary of the town he is safe and wins the game."

So one could go on showing how certain desirable qualities of character are deliberately developed, how abilities are trained, and how all is done within the boy's own world.

It may be asked, "But what has this got to do with citizenship ? What about the powers of the Borough Council, and the local drainage system ?" The answer is that without sound character there can be no sound citizenship, and if anyone wants to know what are the powers of the Borough Council, the facts can be looked up in a few minutes, but you cannot develop a quality of character through exercising it for a few minutes ; it is a matter of years. Scouting goes further than this ; it deliberately aims at training boys to look after their own affairs so that later on they will be able to look after their public affairs. This is perhaps the most distinctive contribution of the Scout method and has already been referred to as the Patrol System. B.-P. went so far as to say, "The dividing of

SEA SCOUTS SERVING AT A MOBILE CANTEEN

the boys into permanent Patrols of from six to eight and treating them
as separate units each under its own responsible leader, is the key to
success with a Troop." Why ?

First of all because the group of six to eight is the right gang-size
for the boy of eleven or twelve to grasp ; it is not so big that he loses his
identity and usefulness—for it is absolutely essential that he should feel
that he is a working member of the gang. So he learns on a small scale
to work and play with others. At the same time he sees the importance
of obedience (even if he argues afterwards) to his Patrol Leader. This
matter of the size of the unit may seem unimportant to those who do not
know boys ; actually it is fundamental. His gang must not be so small
as to be ineffective as a team, and it must not be so big that he feels
insignificant.

COOKING OVER AN OPEN FIRE

Most Patrols meet apart from the Troop once a week, and the Patrol in Council is another stage in citizenship training; here are discussed, on of course a simple scale but with all the seriousness of boyhood, the plans for the Patrol activities, for taking part, perhaps, in an Inter-Patrol Competition or Challenge, or for a week-end camp.

The Patrol Leader gets a particularly valuable training, for, in a good Troop, he is given as much responsibility as possible. B.-P. put great

FRUIT PICKING IN WAR TIME

stress on this as he had learned by experience that apparently dull youths can be stimulated by being given responsible work. All the Patrol Leaders meet together once a week, as has already been mentioned, at a Court of Honour ; the name indicates its origin. It was at first meant to be a disciplinary body to deal with breaches of rules ; but this use is rarely called into play. The Court now plans the activities of the Troop and watches the progress of the Scouts.

The degree to which the Scoutmaster guides the Patrol Leaders varies according to the experience of the Troop and to the willingness of the Scoutmaster to sit back and allow minor failures for the sake of the training-value of the system. How successful this has proved has now been fully demonstrated in two wars, for many a Troop has kept going under its Court of Honour when the Scoutmasters have been called to Service. Not all Troops have done this, and where there has been failure it can, as often as not, be attributed to the Scoutmaster who would not allow the Patrol Leaders to grow wise through experience, either because he was too timid, or because he was too selfish and domineering.

Here then we have a practical training in community life—boys learning through the rough and tumble of experience how to work and play together and how to manage their own affairs. Later on as Rover Scouts they may learn more of the meaning of the Patrol System and see how the same ideas can be applied to the life of the citizen. The Rover may become, in time, a member of his Town Council, or just a Committee man of the tennis club, or be content to live as a good neighbour ; whichever he does, Scouting will have helped him to play his part with greater confidence than he might otherwise have shown.

It would be easy to write at considerable length about other aspects of this citizenship training, but there is only space for describing one more. Scouting has done much to develop a love of the country side and a pride in its right treatment. At the beginning of the century this form of patriotism was not recognised as important. B.-P. took the boys out into the country to camp and to play their games and to learn woodcraft. To them it has always been just great fun—a sort of Robinson Crusoeish business ; but all the time they were learning to know and love the fields, and woods, and streams. It is not done by "Nature rambles," but by putting the boy in such a situation that he needs to know certain things. To take one example : to be expert at making an outdoor fire it is essential to be able to recognise wood from various trees and to know the value of each as fuel—so comes the need for knowing the names of trees.

Camping itself, in 1908, was an activity largely limited to those stalwarts who founded the Camping Club—of which B.-P. was President for many years. Scouting did a great deal to popularise camping—not so much the large camp run on military lines, as the small intimate camp. Out of camping developed trekking and hiking ; the latter has become a national pastime and has led to the establishment of Youth Hostels, all developing a keener love of the countryside and a greater knowledge of one's own land.

AN INTERNATIONAL MOOT IN SCOTLAND, 1939

Rover Scouts from Egypt, Rhodesia, England, Scotland, Armenia, Irak, Norway and Australia

A KING'S SCOUT TALKING TO BOY SCOUTS FROM GIBRALTAR, LONDON 1941

This King's Scout afterwards toured Canada and the U.S.A., with three others, to describe their experiences in Air Raids.

CHEERFUL SCOUTS
Pen drawing by Lord Baden-Powell

NATIONAL SERVICE

Scouting is a pre-citizenship and not a pre-military form of training. The fact that in war-time many a man is grateful for his experiences as a Scout is a tribute not to the specifically military value of the training, but to the broad general foundation it provides for all types of national service. It is to be hoped that the old charge of being a disguised form of militarism will never again be made against the Movement ; its scope is much wider and more permanent than that. The qualities of resourcefulness and adaptability which men have found so valuable in warfare, are equally valuable in peace.

Peace, however, does not offer such spectacular opportunities for service as war—that is one of the tragic aspects of our modern civilisation. Yet Boy Scouts have always managed to find service jobs to do, sometimes of a very simple character but none the less valuable.

When War broke out in 1914, the Movement was barely six years old and no one would have been surprised if it had collapsed. Lord Kitchener at once saw its value. He called for the service of Scouts as coastguards, as messengers, and orderlies. His confidence proved well founded.

In 1939 the scale of the war produced a different situation, but once again Scouts were quickly finding service jobs of all kinds. A very long list—containing nearly 200 items—could be given of the different kinds of work they undertook. A.R.P. naturally made use of the services of Boy Scouts and the records of the boys' devotion to duty and heroism in danger makes inspiring reading. No one claims that they are braver than others, but it can be confidently said that a youngster who has been trained as a Boy Scout is more likely to keep his head in times of emergency than a boy with no such training. It should be remembered that a Scout is not only told to be of service to his fellows, but he is trained so that he can render practical service. Great emphasis has always been put on this preparedness, and from the beginning Scouts who have proved equal to emergencies, such as drowning, street accidents, and so on, have received awards in the form of medals or certificates. It would be possible to fill many pages with stories of heroism and endurance, but the whole youth of the nation has come through the ordeal of fire with a proud record and it would be invidious to select a special group for emphasis.

One story, however, is worth telling as a good illustration of the Scout method. A group of Scouts in a West Country town volunteered for fire service. Soon they became the proud guardians of a trailer pump. They practised regularly until they felt thoroughly prepared. For months it looked as though their services would not be needed. Then one night in May 1941 the call came. They were in charge of an objective which they knew would be bombed again and again. One of the team met with an accident during the early part of the raid. He was knocked unconscious and so did not join his fellows on the call. Recovering, he intended to follow them, but saw a building on fire. He went to the assistance of three women whose garage was ablaze and fought the fire with buckets of water. He then climbed to the roof to cut loose a section of it in order to save the rest of the building. A second member, after doing some splendid work with the pump at the main fire, was laying another hose when he received some shell splinter in his back, which, coming out below his stomach, made a bad wound ; but he made no complaint, his only concern being for the safety of the others and of his people. The leader, aged eighteen, took the most dangerous position alone, and when offered relief, he declined it, saying : "You are none too strong and have some heavy work ; I am all right." A minute or so later two bombs straddled the fire and this boy was killed. His brother was injured in the arm and leg but made no mention of these injuries : it was thus that he came to be sent to turn off the water, the hose being now damaged beyond use, and also to fetch the stretcher party. He dragged himself for half a mile through the height of the blitz but had to give up and was taken away in an ambulance.

It can never be known how far Scouting has helped the hundreds of thousands of boys who have passed through its ranks, to become more efficient soldiers, sailors and airmen.

"THE MORE WE GET TOGETHER"
Stalin, Roosevelt, Chiang Kai Shek and Churchill
Cartoon by E. H. Shepard, from *Punch*, 1942

In July 1942, Mr. Churchill sent the following message to the Boy Scouts :

"I first met B.-P. many years before the birth of the Scout Movement. He was a man of character, vision, and enthusiasm, and he passed these qualities on to the Movement which has played, and is playing, an important part in moulding the character of our race. Sturdiness, neighbourliness, practical competence, love of country, and above all, in these times, indomitable resolve, daring, and enterprise in the face of the enemy, these are the hallmarks of a Scout. . . 'Be Prepared' to stand up faithfully for Right and Truth however the winds may blow."

Winston S. Churchill

OFF TO CAMP BY BARGE

THE END OF A PERIOD

The coming of war in 1939 and the Founder's death in 1941 mark the end of a period in the Boy Scout Movement.

It has been given to few men to see the fruits of their labours to the degree which B.-P. enjoyed. He was fifty years old when the Brownsea Island camp was held in 1907. A year later the Movement took shape, and twenty-one years after that, the Coming-of-Age Jamboree was held at Arrowe Park, Birkenhead.

The first of these vast International Camps was held in 1920, and B.-P. suggested the name : he disclaimed all knowledge of the origin of the word ; it had stuck in his memory and as he said "What else could you call it ?"

Jamborees were held every four years and the countries so far which have acted as hosts have been Great Britain, Denmark, Hungary and Holland. The last was held in 1937. It was an *annus mirabilis* for B.-P.

He was eighty ; his own country bestowed on him the Order of Merit ; France gave him the Grand Cordon of the Legion of Honour ; from America came the Wateler Peace Prize. At the Jamboree in Holland, 28,000 Scouts of thirty-one nations camped together. Many realised as they saw the familiar slight, wiry figure, and heard his strong voice that this might prove his last Jamboree.

His last years were spent in Kenya ; almost to the end he was active— watching animal life and painting pictures of the scenes he loved so well, keeping up his enormous correspondence, and throwing out from time to time fresh ideas for the two Movements he had founded. He died on 8th January 1941, and he rests in the Africa which was his second homeland ; Mount Kenya looks down on his grave.

He was succeeded as Chief Scout by Lord Somers, K.C.M.G., D.S.O., M.C., who had been Deputy Chief Scout for several years. Unhappily his period of office was all too brief. He quickly proved how worthy a successor he was to B.-P., but after many months of illness he died on 14th July, 1944. Lord Rowallan, M.C., was appointed Chief Scout in February, 1945.

LORD ROWALLAN
The present Chief Scout

THE FUTURE

What of the future ? It is rash to take up the role of prophet, but a few possibilities are worth considering.

As long as there is need for the type of training Scouting gives, it will have its part to play provided the State does not usurp all the fields of service at present open to voluntary effort. Scouting would be killed the day it became a State-controlled Movement or one to which boys were compelled to belong. It is difficult to exaggerate the moral value of the fact that a Boy Scout *of his own free will* makes a solemn promise before his fellows that he will do his best to do his duty to God and the King, and to obey the Scout Law. He undertakes freely to make a real effort to live up to a clearly defined standard. This is important in a world where standards have been so widely held up to scorn.

In addition to the boys, there are the adults (some 40,000 of them in 1938 with a similar number in the Guide Movement), who gladly give up their leisure time to the Movement. It will be a sad day—should it ever come—when such a field for community service is closed to the volunteer in favour of paid full-time leaders. Some exclaim that this is not possible, but there have been hints here and there that some would like to see all this volunteer youth work tidied up and "co-ordinated" into a well-planned scheme. The loss to national character would be considerable, for this kind of voluntary social service by men and women of all types has its roots deep down in the community life.

Left to itself, the Boy Scout Movement can play a useful part in the Service of Youth. It does not depend on State support and it has always refused to accept any public grants which might hamper its free development ; so far there has been no clash in this matter, but the steady encroachment of State control in many fields calls for constant watchfulness.

Plans are now being developed to strengthen a weak section in the chain of training. Special care is needed with the boys of the 15-18 age group. In the past too many have slipped away on going to work and have lost the steadying influence of Scouting at the period when it was most needed. Time alone can show whether the scheme for the Senior Scouts will meet the need.

Scouting should become a stronger and stronger bond between the countries and peoples of the British Empire. The tie has always been a close one, but the distance of the greater part of the Empire from Great Britain has meant far too few personal contacts except at the great Jamborees.

The presence of so many former Scouts on service in this country during the war did much to draw all together in a more firmly knit brotherhood. Advances in means of transport may be expected to facilitate an

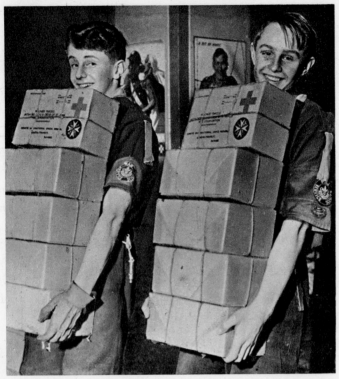

HELPING THE PRISONERS OF WAR PARCELS SCHEME

even closer union such as we all look for.

Scouting has proved particularly successful in some of the less advanced countries of the Empire, where the boys have taken to it with considerable gusto. Here too, then, is an important function which may be expected to develop further.

Finally, there are the possibilities in the field of good relations between all countries. As the largest Youth Movement in the world, the Boy Scouts feel a special responsibility in this matter, though they realise that their efforts are but one small tributary to what must become a vast river of good will if universal brotherhood is to be a reality.

The Scouts International Relief Service sent teams of workers to the Middle East, Greece, Yugoslavia and Italy, and to France, Holland and Germany. Their work was amongst refugees, civilian casualties and those unfortunate people deported by Germany for enforced labour. This very practical expression of "helping others at all times" not only brought

47

succour to those in need, but it has been the means of linking up British Scouting once more with the Movement in other countries. In spite of restrictions and attempted suppression, Scouting has survived and has even been strengthened through adversity. Italy supplies the most striking example of the deep roots Scouting has taken. The Movement was suppressed by the Fascist Government in 1926. Within a few months of liberation, Scouting sprang up again in Sicily, and later throughout Italy. It has never been possible to get a genuine Scout movement established in Germany—perhaps that too may come one day.

The International Bureau, to which recognised national Associations are affiliated, organises a Conference every two years at which matters of common interest can be discussed, and this body may well play a more and more important part in developing this world-wide Movement.

The Movement is obviously not going to lack opportunities for extended service at home, overseas, and abroad. If it is to meet these calls upon it, there will be an ever growing need for adults to come forward to help. There is a great variety of work open to laymen quite apart from the job of training the boys. Instructors, badge examiners, chairmen, treasurers and secretaries—to mention but a few—are all wanted wherever Scouts are found.

The greatest need of all is for young men who will train the boys. Here is a world of service for those who have a vision of the future happiness of their fellow citizens. The boys are there in their hundreds of thousands, waiting for men to come forward with *Scouting for Boys* in their hands and the enthusiasm to put it into practice.

B.-P.'s IDEA OF A SCOUT
Pen drawing by Lord Baden-Powell